1940—1949

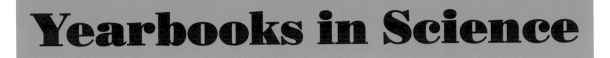

Yearbooks in Science

1940–1949

Nathan Aaseng

Twenty-First Century Books
A Division of Henry Holt and Company
New York

Twenty-First Century Books
A Division of Henry Holt and Company, Inc.
115 West 18th Street
New York, NY 10011

Henry Holt® and colophon are trademarks of
Henry Holt and Company, Inc.
Publishers since 1866

Published in Canada by Fitzhenry & Whiteside Ltd.
195 Allstate Parkway, Markham, Ontario L3R 4T8

Library of Congress Cataloging-in-Publication Data
Yearbooks in science.
p.   cm.
Includes indexes.
Contents: 1900–1919 / Tom McGowen—1920–1929 / David E. Newton—1930–1939 / Nathan Aaseng—1940–1949 / Nathan Aaseng—1950–1959 / Mona Kerby—1960–1969 / Tom McGowen—1970–1979 / Geraldine Marshall Gutfreund—1980–1989 / Robert E. Dunbar—1990 and beyond / Herma Silverstein.
ISBN 0–8050–3431–5 (v. 1)
1. Science—History—20th century—Juvenile literature. 2. Technology—History—20th century—Juvenile literature.
3. Inventions—History—20th century—Juvenile literature. 4. Scientists—20th century—Juvenile literature.
5. Engineers—20th century—Juvenile literature. [1. Science—History—20th century. 2. Technology—History—20th century.]
Q126.4.Y43 1995
609'.04—dc20   95–17485
                                                                                              CIP
                                                                                              AC

ISBN 0–8050–3434–X
First Edition 1995
Printed in Mexico
All first editions are printed on acid-free paper ∞.
10 9 8 7 6 5 4 3 2 1

Cover design by James Sinclair
Interior design by Kelly Soong

Cover photo credits
Background: Mushroom cloud at Nagasaki, © Scott Camazine/Photo Researchers, Inc. **Inset images** (clockwise from top right): Kidney, © Biophoto Associates/Photo Researchers, Inc.; SCUBA symbol designed by James Sinclair; Penicillin, © Michael Siegel/Phototake NYC; Velcro, Dr. Jeremy Burgess/Science Photo Library/Photo Researchers, Inc.; Red blood cells, © Dr. Dennis Kunkel, Phototake NYC; Leaf from a green plant, Comstock.

Photo Credits
p. 11: Dr. Jeremy Burgess/Science Photo Library/Photo Researchers, Inc.; p. 16, 54: SPL/Photo Researchers, Inc.; p. 18: Dr. Harold Agnew (Los Alamos Scientific Library)/SPL/Photo Researchers, Inc.; p. 19: Argonne National Laboratory/Mark Marten/Photo Researchers, Inc.; p. 21: American Institute of Physics/Emilio Segre Visual Archives; p. 22: University of California Lawrence Radiation Laboratory, Berkeley/Photo Researchers, Inc.; p. 24: Los Alamos National Laboratory/SPL/Photo Researchers, Inc.; p. 25: UPI/Bettmann; p. 26: © Scott Camazine/Photo Researchers, Inc.; p. 27: Lawrence Laboratory, Berkeley/courtesy AIP/Emilio Segre Visual Archives; p. 28: © 1980 Jim Goodwin/Photo Researchers, Inc.; p. 32: © Fabian Bachrach/The University of Chicago Library; p. 34: Comstock; p. 36: © Kenneth Eward/BioGrafx/Science Source/Photo Researchers, Inc.; p. 38: Courtesy of the Rockefeller Archive Center; p. 39: CNRI/SPL/Photo Researchers, Inc.; p. 42: Westinghouse Historical Collection; p. 43, 45, 69: The Bettmann Archive; p. 44: Courtesy of Polaroid Corporate Archives; p. 47; Department of Special Collections/Van Pelt-Dietrich Library Center/University of Pennsylvania; p. 50, 52, 57: UPI/Bettmann Newsphotos; p. 55: UPI/Bettmann; p.60: Science Source/Photo Researchrs, Inc.; p. 65: St. Mary's Hospital Medical School/SPL/Photo Researchers, Inc.; p. 70: © Biophoto Associates/Photo Researchers, Inc.; p. 71: © Dr. Dennis Kunkel/Phototake NYC.

To Sunniva and Kristopher

Contents

INTRODUCTION: SCIENCE IN THE SHADOW OF DEATH   9

1   NUCLEAR PHYSICS   15

2   CHEMISTRY   31

3   BIOLOGY   37

4   COMMUNICATION AND INFORMATION   41

5   TRANSPORTATION   51

6   SPACE AND THE UPPER ATMOSPHERE   59

7   HEALTH AND MEDICINE   63

FURTHER READING   75

INDEX   77

Introduction

SCIENCE IN THE SHADOW OF DEATH

The decade of the 1940s roared onto the stage of history on the wings of war, destruction, and unspeakable terror. The Axis powers of Nazi Germany, Italy, and Japan opened the decade by hurling every weapon in their powerful arsenals in an attempt to dominate the nations of the world. Their actions brought about the most widespread, devastating conflict the world has ever known. The cyclone of madness spun out of control as it brought about the systematic mass murders of Jews and others targeted for extinction by ruthless leaders such as Adolf Hitler and Joseph Stalin.

World War II consumed half the decade. During that time, scientists, like virtually everyone else, labored under its grim shadow. Scientists in many fields were forced to set aside their work in progress so that they could join the war effort. The warring nations turned to scientists to use every bit of cunning, every innovation of technology, to guarantee ultimate victory.

So it was that scientific development during the 1940s focused on military superiority. Most of the research breakthroughs of the decade and the practical inventions that resulted had to do with warfare. For example, Germany employed the talents of scientists and engineers to develop and build more than 115,000 military aircraft and thousands of deadly missiles during the war. On the other side, when Japanese forces captured the United States' sources of natural rubber in the South Pacific, American chemists and engineers responded by creating a synthetic replacement for rubber.

In the end, the science and technology of the Allied forces outraced the science and technology of the Axis powers. American and British advances in radar detection, begun in the 1930s, evened the odds when the British were reeling against the superior German air force. Computer advances provided the Allies with a huge advantage by cracking Germany's top secret code, giving advance warning of what the Germans planned to do and when.

Fortunately, most of the scientific advances made in the pursuit of war could be turned to peaceful uses as well. The development of radar techniques for locating enemy aircraft and predicting storms that might affect military operations proved valuable in both peacetime navigation and weather forecasting. Scientific experimentation with new materials such as plastics and metal alloys that could build better engines of war proved valuable in the creation of thousands of durable consumer goods. The invention of complex calculating machines to break enemy codes and to improve the accuracy of artillery fire branched off into computers that have revolutionized the way we process and tabulate information.

Unfortunately, the scientific community's most memorable accomplishment of the 1940s ushered in a new terror that made conventional warfare look like a water fight in comparison. By unlocking the secrets of tiny particles of matter, scientists triggered a race among physicists and engineers eager to find a way to harness this power. The Americans won the race. The bombs they developed sealed Japan's defeat.

With the development of nuclear bombs, scientists made possible for the first time in history the instant annihilation of the human species. Any peaceful benefits of this unleashing of the atom, such as nuclear power plants for generating electricity, have paled in comparison to the threat this new technology has posed.

One of the most important changes the war imposed on the scientific community was to shift creative genius from Eastern Europe, particularly Germany, to the United States. Prior to the 1940s, Germany was the undisputed center of scientific research. The United States was little more than a spectator to major developments in most scientific fields, especially physics.

The racial policies of the Nazi government erased Germany's scientific advantage. Many of Eastern Europe's top scientists were Jews who fled Nazi persecution and ended up in the United States. Their expertise could well have provided Germany with the technological superiority to win the war. Instead, these brilliant scientists worked their wonders to defeat the Nazi government.

The immigration of top scientists woke up a previously sluggish American effort in scientific research. For example, in 1920, the five largest American pharmaceutical companies employed a total of twenty-six research chemists. By the dawn of the 1940s, those same companies sponsored nearly 150 full-time chemists probing the frontiers of their science. With this influx of talent and interest, American scientists not only developed the first atomic bombs but began to dominate the Nobel Prizes in the sciences for decades to come.

The 1940s also completed the transfer of scientific and technological research from individuals and small laboratories to huge, multimillion-dollar projects. There were, of course, exceptions—lone individuals who made their mark on the world. In 1948, Swiss engineer Georges de Mestral took his dog for a walk in the woods. When he returned home, he had to spend a good deal of time cleaning out the cockleburs that had lodged in his dog's hair. While doing so, he conceived the idea of using the annoying example of the cocklebur for a useful purpose. So it was that de Mestral invented the Velcro fastener, which is used in thousands of products today.

But for the most part, science and invention began to follow the example of the enormous Manhattan Project, which produced the atomic bomb. This U.S. government project was so complex and difficult that it required the efforts of hundreds of top physicists. Project leaders constructed entire new cities, housing as many as 75,000 workers, and spent billions of dollars before they reached their goal.

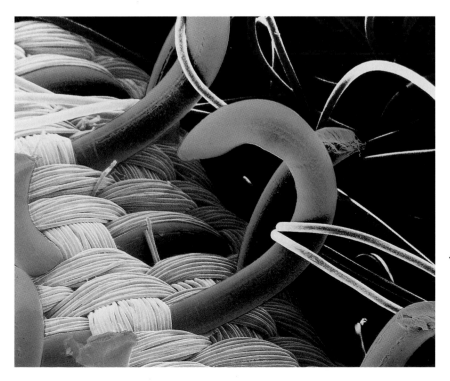

This is a micrograph—a picture taken through a microscope—of Velcro, now a common fastener. Velcro is manufactured in two separate pieces, one with a hooked surface (left) *and the other with a smooth surface covered with loops* (right).

While most current research efforts are nowhere near the scale of the Manhattan Project, big science became the standard way of tackling scientific research. During the 1940s, governments made large amounts of money available for important projects. Giant corporations such as the Bell Telephone Company set up and funded large research teams of their own. Many of the most influential innovations of the future would come about through such massive cooperative efforts. As a result, it has become increasingly difficult to tell what individuals are responsible for such inventions as the computer and lasers, for producing atomic energy, and for landing an astronaut on the moon.

Not every scientific pursuit of the 1940s had to do with war and weapons. As both biologists and chemists followed their separate trail of clues, searching for a better understanding of the human body, they found that the trails eventually came together. By combining the two areas of study, biochemists in the 1940s began to unravel ancient mysteries such as how plants use sunlight to create food and how genetic traits are passed from one generation to another.

Research by physicists into the properties of solid substances known as semiconductors brought the discovery of transistors. This in turn sparked a miniaturization revolution that eventually made such equipment as computers and portable radios practical.

Prior to World War II, science had played a minor role in improving medical treatment. But with the discovery of an expanding arsenal of antibiotics in the 1940s, doctors stepped up their attacks on diseases. People suddenly looked to science for cures to the medical problems that ailed them.

Science and technology of the 1940s brought about drastic changes in modern lifestyles. In 1940, no household had a television. Phonographic records contained only a few minutes' worth of music per side. Few ordinary citizens ever traveled by airplane. By the end of the decade, television, recorded music, and commercial air flight were well on the way to becoming important elements of modern life.

Perhaps the most important impact of scientific achievement in the 1940s was to inspire awe in the average citizen. By opening up and harnessing the unimaginable power of the atom, scientists seemed to have proved that there was no limit to what they could do. With the end of the war came optimism that science would be able to provide unlimited benefits. New drugs promised an end to many kinds of deadly diseases. In 1946, Vincent Schaefer found that frozen carbon dioxide could cause supercool water vapor to precipitate. His initial experiments in cloud seeding led to dreams of worldwide climate control. At the same time, nuclear power plants promised unlimited power. One top scientist declared that nuclear power would soon make electricity "too cheap to meter."

Few people in the 1940s listened to a farsighted writer named Aldo Leopold, who warned that there were limits to what science could accomplish. Humans should not tinker with the world and upset and reshape it without thinking about the consequences. There were dangers, said Leopold, in playing carelessly with the natural world.

In the decades that followed, people became cautious and even skeptical toward claims of the all-conquering ability of scientists. Nuclear power did not make electricity too cheap to meter, and in fact brought enormously expensive waste disposal problems. Climate control through cloud seeding has never been developed. The environmental movement mushroomed when people saw that Leopold had a point in warning about the limits of technology.

But our world remains dependent on science. Lifestyles change according to the latest findings and creations of science. The big push for science and technology generated in the desperate world of the 1940s continues to this day.

1

NUCLEAR PHYSICS

When scientists pried open the atom in the 1930s, the stunning secrets they uncovered catapulted nuclear physics into the starring role in the science world. Physicists were dealing with a possible source of energy and power beyond anyone's imagination.

A series of important developments in the 1930s enticed physicists to chase in earnest after this incredible power. First, Frédéric and Irène Joliot-Curie of France discovered artificial radioactivity. In other words, they found a way to make elements so unstable that these elements would shed some of their subatomic particles. In so doing, elements would actually change into other elements.

Ernest Lawrence of the United States then provided a tool for firing particles at atoms. His cyclotron increased the speed at which scientists could accelerate electrons until they traveled fast enough to overcome the strong repulsive force of the nucleus. Scientists found that they could create a variety of changes in atoms by bombarding them with these small particles.

James Chadwick of England shed further light on the nature of the atomic nucleus by proving the existence of a subatomic particle called a neutron. Neutrons proved to be more effective bullets than electrons. Not only were they much larger than electrons, but because they had no electrical charge, they did not have to overcome the repulsive force of the nucleus.

Italian physicist Enrico Fermi began playing around with these newly discovered particles. He tried to create an element that did not exist in nature by shooting a neutron into the nucleus of uranium, the heaviest element in existence. His experiments caused the uranium to turn radioactive. This convinced Fermi that he had succeeded in creating an element heavier than uranium.

But further analysis by German physical chemist Otto Hahn and his col-

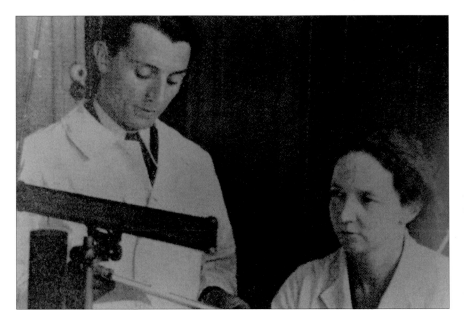

Frédéric and Irène Joliot-Curie discovered artificial radioactivity in 1934 and were awarded the Nobel Prize in chemistry in 1935.

league, Austrian physicist Lise Meitner, showed that something even stranger had happened. Fermi had actually split some of the uranium atoms into two pieces to form two smaller elements.

The news that atoms could be split especially intrigued physicists because of the amount of energy released during the split. Since atoms are so small, the energy released by the breakup or "fission" of a few atoms would hardly be noticed. But if a couple of ounces of uranium, containing billions of atoms, could be split at once, the energy release would be tremendous.

This fascinating discovery did not appear to be particularly useful, though, because there was no practical way to fire enough particles at once to split all that uranium. But eight months before the start of the 1940s, the Joliot-Curies made an earthshaking discovery. They found that when they bombarded uranium with neutrons, the splitting neutrons released more neutrons.

Most of these loose neutrons were soaked up by impurities in the uranium compounds. Physicists, however, recognized that the Joliot-Curies' discovery hinted at the possibility of a chain reaction: one neutron would split an atom, causing the release of two more neutrons. These would split two more atoms, each causing the release of two neutrons for a total of four, and so on. This chain reaction could build so rapidly that an enormous amount of energy would be released in less than one-millionth of a second.

The Dreadful Significance of Nuclear Chain Reactions

At the beginning of the 1940s, this discovery produced conflicting emotions of enthusiasm and horror in physicists. Yet it attracted them like moths to a light. The brilliant American J. Robert Oppenheimer spoke for many physicists when he recalled, "Ever since the discovery of nuclear fission, the possibility of powerful explosions based on it had been much on my mind."

Such a possibility was also much on the mind of American physicist Leo Szilard, and it scared him. At first, he tried to stop the drive toward nuclear fission by asking people like Fermi and the Joliot-Curies not to publish their findings. When that failed, he tried to make sure that the right people got their hands on nuclear power first. Szilard and renowned physicist Albert Einstein, another European scientist who had sought refuge in the United States, sent a letter warning U.S. President Franklin Roosevelt that "extremely powerful bombs of a new type may thus be constructed," and urged him to sponsor a government effort to build the bomb before the Nazis accomplished the feat.

Roosevelt did not act immediately on the warning. At first, the United States considered development of a nuclear bomb a long shot and therefore gave it low priority. As an example, the military was suspicious enough of defecting physicists to deny them clearance to work on projects such as radar. Yet it had no qualms about letting these foreign-born experts work on problems having to do with the atomic bomb.

But in 1940, two other refugee scientists, R. E. Peierls and Otto Frisch, arrived in Great Britain with a warning similar to that of Szilard and Einstein. The British government brought together a commission of experts to study the situation. In July 1941, this commission issued a report confirming that an atomic bomb carrying a force equal to several thousand tons of TNT could be built. It estimated that a concentrated effort by any of the dominant countries in the world could produce such a weapon within three to four years.

A Hungarian Jew who had fled his homeland because of Nazi persecution, Szilard knew firsthand how desperately important it was for someone to beat the Nazis to the bomb.

The British forwarded this report to Vannevar Bush, director of the U.S. Office of Scientific Research and Development. Bush then recommended a full-scale, top priority effort to produce an atomic bomb. General Leslie Groves was assigned to head this secret effort, known as the Manhattan Project.

ACHIEVING CRITICAL MASS

Enrico Fermi, who had fled Italy for fear of its Fascist government, took charge of producing a chain reaction. Working at the University of Chicago, Fermi constructed an "atomic pile" made up of layers of graphite blocks alternating with chunks of uranium and uranium oxide. Flying neutrons did not affect the carbon atoms in the graphite but were slowed down when they collided with these atoms. At slower speeds, these neutrons were more likely to split uranium atoms. Removable cadmium rods were also inserted into the pile. This material could absorb neutrons and so helped Fermi control the chain reaction. He hoped to start the reaction by removing the rods, which would increase the number of free neutrons. If the chain reaction became too intense, Fermi could insert the cadmium rods to sop up the neutrons and slow or stop the pile.

When the effort to produce an atomic bomb became a top priority, Enrico Fermi took charge of the team assigned to produce the world's first nuclear chain reaction.

The key to the operation was finding the "critical mass." This was the amount of fissioning uranium needed to produce more neutrons than were being lost or captured by other elements. Fermi kept building the pile higher, adding more uranium until he was close to the critical mass.

On December 2, 1942, six weeks after starting work on the atomic pile, Fermi was ready for the test. No one knew for certain what would happen if they achieved a chain reaction, or whether there really was any way of controlling such an explosive event. A courageous "suicide squad" of scientists mounted a platform above the pile, ready to pour cadmium salt liquid on the pile if the reaction should blow out of control. The only man on the floor of the room was George Weil, whose job was to start the reaction by removing a cadmium rod.

At 3:45 P.M., Fermi and his team looked on with sweaty palms and pounding hearts as Weil did his job. Geiger counters that measured the amount of radioactivity in the pile began clicking furiously. The experiment worked. Fermi not only achieved his chain reaction but was able to shut it off without catastrophe. The scientists celebrated by drinking wine from paper cups. But they were well aware of the enormous impact of what they had done. One of

This painting depicts the first successful nuclear chain reaction. The suicide squad is shown at top right, and George Weil is at bottom center.

The phone call in which physicist Arthur Compton reported the results of Fermi's experiment to his colleague, James Conant at Harvard University, illustrates the strict secrecy that surrounded the Manhattan Project:

> Compton: The Italian Navigator has reached the new world.
> Conant: And how did he find the natives?
> Compton: Very friendly.

them commented, "We knew that with the advent of the chain reaction, the world would never be the same again."

URANIUM-238 VERSUS URANIUM-235

The next step in producing an atomic bomb was uranium enrichment. Uranium occurs in two forms in nature: U-235 and U-238. Physicists had determined that only the U-235 form would sustain a chain reaction. U-238 would only absorb neutrons and so interfere with the chain reaction. Unfortunately, only about 0.7 percent of the uranium in the world was U-235. Furthermore, U-235 and U-238 were so similar that separating them was extremely difficult.

Philip Abelson and Harold Urey were the physicists most responsible for creating the gaseous diffusion technique of uranium enrichment. Abelson pointed the team in the right direction by suggesting they first convert uranium into uranium hexafluoride, a liquid that could be easily evaporated.

The uranium gas formed by evaporation could then be passed through a long tube that contained small holes. The difference in weight between the U-235 gas and the U-238 gas was tiny but just enough so that the slightly lighter U-235 gas would arrive first and diffuse through the holes before the U-238. This would provide enough separation to obtain very slightly enriched uranium.

Urey was put in charge of designing the system that would make gaseous diffusion practical. In reality, there was nothing practical about it. Only an emergency wartime effort could have provided scientists with a 2,000,000-square-foot (180,000-square-meter) building, more than 70,000 workers, and a new city (Oak Ridge, Tennessee) to house these workers.

But even that colossal effort did not seem to be enough to solve the problems. By the spring of 1943, the plant was still producing only a dusting of enriched material. Ernest Lawrence's method of using electromagnets to separate the two uranium isotopes was proving equally costly and difficult. A third method of thermal diffusion, using heat to cause the slightly lighter U-235 to rise faster than U-238, was also tried. None of these methods was producing enough enriched uranium to fashion into a bomb.

While physicists were scratching their heads over this problem, an unexpected alternative became available. In 1940, Abelson and Edwin McMillan had repeated some of Fermi's experiments bombarding uranium with neutrons. They found that these experiments produced some unusual, short-lived radiation. In tracking down the source of this radiation, they discovered that while some uranium split when struck by a neutron, other uranium atoms simply held on to the incoming neutron. This changed the uranium into a different element, which is what Fermi had been trying to do in the first place. McMillan and Abelson named this new element neptunium (neptunium being the element beyond uranium just as Neptune is the planet beyond Uranus).

An aerial photograph taken in 1945 clearly shows the size of the Oak Ridge National Laboratory.

The Discovery of Plutonium

Because neptunium decayed in just a couple of days, it had no practical use. But later that same year, Glenn Seaborg continued efforts to create new elements beyond uranium. Working at the University of California at Berkeley, Seaborg discovered that neutron bombardment of uranium oxide also produced an even heavier element. Continuing with the trend of naming elements for distant planets, he named this element plutonium.

Plutonium lasted longer than neptunium, and scientists could study its characteristics. Although the amount of plutonium available for research would have fit on the head of a pin, with room to spare, physicists were able to use this small sample to calculate that plutonium could produce a powerful chain reaction. Concerned about the problems with obtaining U-235, the Manhattan Project leaders turned to plutonium as an alternative.

They constructed atomic piles that produced several grams of plutonium per month.

The project then set up a large reactor at a remote site in Hanford, Washington, to produce enough plutonium to build a bomb. As in Oak Ridge, thousands of workers were brought in to run the plant.

The Hanford plutonium plant began operation in September 1944. In March 1945, the uranium diffusion process also began producing acceptable quantities of enriched U-235. Physicists then had two sources of explosive power with which to build their bomb.

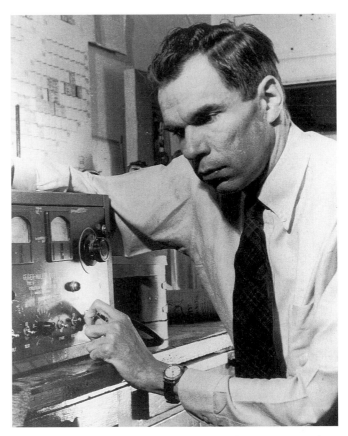

Glenn Seaborg is shown working in his laboratory in 1946. He is counting a radioactive sample in a Geiger counter.

Seaborg continued to bombard uranium with neutrons after the war in an effort to create even heavier artificial elements. He created six artificial elements beyond plutonium. None of them had any practical value.

BUILDING THE BOMB

The task of actually constructing the explosive device fell to a team headed by J. Robert Oppenheimer. In autumn of 1942, Oppenheimer suggested setting up a new, top secret laboratory at a former boys' boarding school in Los Alamos, located in a remote area of New Mexico. Since the team did not know at that stage which source of nuclear power they would be using, they had to design two bombs, one to work with plutonium and one with uranium.

The main problem in designing an atomic bomb was how to reach critical mass at the proper time. How could you pack a bomb with enough uranium or plutonium to produce a chain reaction without having the reaction go off too soon?

The uranium bomb proved the easier of the two to design. The final product contained a piece of uranium-235 just short of the critical mass needed to start the reaction. Another section of the bomb contained a smaller piece of U-235. The bomb could be detonated with a small explosive device that fired the smaller piece into the larger piece, thus putting it over the critical mass. The technique was straightforward enough that scientists did not feel the need to waste the U-235 material on a test bomb.

This method of detonation, however, did not work with plutonium. Physicists and explosive experts found that they had to use an "implosion" technique. An implosion is the opposite of an explosion. Instead of causing particles to explode outward, it drives particles inward toward a very small center. A core of plutonium just below the critical mass was placed in the center of the bomb. This was surrounded by powerful explosives arranged in such a way that they would compress the plutonium into a superdense state that would cause the chain reaction to begin.

No one knew for sure if this implosion could be designed precisely enough to produce an atomic blast. Oppenheimer's team chose a stretch of desert at Alamogordo, New Mexico, to test a plutonium bomb. On July 16, 1945, they placed the bomb on a 100-foot- (30-meter-) tall steel tower at a place they named Zero Hill. The detonating device was wired to a control center embedded in the desert 9 miles (14 kilometers) away, where scientists anxiously awaited the moment of truth.

At 5:30 A.M., a brilliant sheet of light ripped through the sky. Observers felt a tremendous shock, followed by a hot hurricane of wind and an explosion so powerful it was heard in Amarillo, Texas, 450 miles (720 kilometers) away. A mushroom cloud of smoke rose 7 miles (11 kilometers) into the air.

The test was successful beyond even the expectations of the scientists. They had predicted a blast equal to 5,000 tons (4,500 metric tons) of TNT. The explosion was measured at closer to 20,000 tons (18,000 metric tons) of TNT. The heat from the bomb melted sand into green glass for 1,000 feet (305 meters) in every direction.

The world's first atomic bomb was photographed in place at the top of its support tower just prior to detonation on July 16, 1945.

FACING THE CONSEQUENCES

Once physicists had built such a terrible weapon, they had to consider whether they really ought to use it. Oppenheimer, Fermi, Lawrence, and Compton met with military leaders to discuss this question. By this time, Germany had surrendered. The United States and its allies had overwhelmed Japan's military forces and had driven them from the lands they had conquered. American military leaders were now planning to invade Japan itself. Japanese forces fought courageously and stubbornly, preferring death to surrender. This meant that the invasion was certain to cost hundreds of thousands of lives on both sides.

The scientists and the military dismissed the idea that a mere demonstration of the atomic bomb would persuade the Japanese to surrender. They decided that use of the weapon was the only alternative to a long and bloody invasion. On August 6, 1945, the B-29 bomber *Enola Gay* dropped a uranium

The crew of the Enola Gay *included pilot Colonel Paul Tibbets. He is in the center of this group, in front of the propeller, wearing a shirt and cap.*

bomb on the city of Hiroshima. Three days later, Americans hit Nagasaki with a plutonium bomb. The cities were leveled and more than 200,000 Japanese died.

Prior to this time, scientific laboratories had been largely free of moral issues and questions. They performed their experiments and reported their results in the objective, detached manner of science. But the destruction caused by the atomic bomb showed that scientists had become too powerful, too influential in determining the fate of the world to ignore the moral consequences of their research. From this moment on, science would become

Oppenheimer could not escape feelings of guilt over his role in creating nuclear weapons. Although he had supported the decision to use the bomb against Japan, he later told President Harry Truman, "I feel we have blood on our hands." In 1962, he said, "My own feeling is that if the bombs were to be used, there could have been more effective warning and much less wanton killing."

increasingly involved in controversial moral questions involving the creation of life, medical issues, and environmental concerns.

The moral questions involved in scientific weapons research intensified during the later 1940s. When the Americans achieved success with their atomic bomb, scientists warned that other countries would eventually have such weapons. They forecast that the Soviet Union would need less than five years to construct its own bomb.

Sure enough, just over a year after the bombing of Hiroshima, the Soviets took an important first step when they achieved a nuclear chain reaction. On August 29, 1949, right on schedule, the Soviets secretly exploded an atomic bomb.

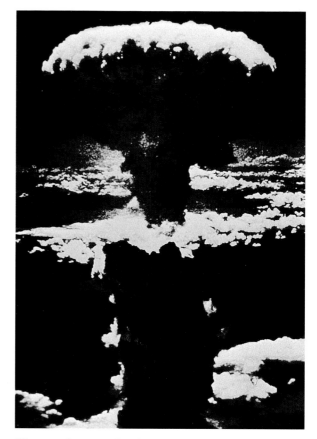

The mushroom cloud created by the bomb dropped on Nagasaki on August 9, 1945

When President Truman announced that event to the world a month later, American scientists faced a new dilemma. The Soviet Union and the United States were fast becoming mortal enemies. Should the United States pursue plans to create even more terrible bombs?

THE HYDROGEN BOMB

For a number of years, physicists had spoken of the possibility of a weapon a thousand times more powerful than the bombs dropped on Japan. The proposed bomb was based on nuclear fusion, which works in exactly the opposite manner as the uranium or plutonium fission bomb.

In nuclear fission, energy is released when very large atoms are split. In fusion, energy is released when small atoms are combined. This is the manner in which stars, including the sun, generate their stupendous power. The fusion bomb called for a method of fusing two very light hydrogen atoms into the heavier helium atom. Scientists discovered that such atoms could be fused at temperatures greater than 100,000,000°F (55,555,538°C). Such temperatures were previously unthinkable.

However, the center of an exploding nuclear fission bomb could get that hot and many scientists believed such a bomb could be built. In fact, American physicists had been engaged in low-key research into the possibility for seven years, since before the first atomic bomb was ever built.

The Soviets' success in building an atomic bomb spurred sudden interest among those who worried that the United States was in danger of losing its military superiority. They proposed a crash program for developing the hydrogen bomb.

This time, even many of the scientists who had been instrumental in developing the atomic bomb spoke out against the project. Enrico Fermi said, "It is clear that the use of such a weapon cannot be justified on any ethical ground." He declared the hydrogen bomb "an evil thing, considered in any light."

Oppenheimer agreed with Fermi. He believed that hydrogen bomb research would automatically provoke the Soviets into creating their own thermonuclear weapons. Besides being a terrible waste of money and resources, this arms race would make the world a

Edward Teller argued in favor of the creation of a thermonuclear bomb.

very dangerous place in which to live. He believed the security of the United States would not be threatened even if the United States backed out of further weapons developments and the Soviets went ahead and developed a thermonuclear bomb. He pointed out that the atomic weapons in the U.S. arsenal were already terrible enough to discourage any nation from attacking.

On the other side of the argument was physicist Edward Teller. Teller distrusted the Soviets, especially after they took over the country of Hungary, where Teller had been born. Teller argued that the refusal of the United States to develop a thermonuclear weapons program would reduce the nation to a second-class world power. He accused people such as Oppenheimer of trying to "stop the progress of science."

Teller won the argument. In 1949, President Truman authorized a pro-

The enormous size of America's first hydrogen bomb is evident in this photograph.

gram to develop the hydrogen bomb. That decision triggered a costly nuclear arms race. Teller and his group secretly developed the principles on which the hydrogen bomb was based. The United States successfully tested such a bomb in 1952. The Soviets matched that a few years later. The arms race was a dominant issue in world politics and continued until the collapse of the Soviet Union in the late 1980s, by which time both sides had enough weapons to destroy the earth many times over.

2

CHEMISTRY

Radioactivity played a key role in chemistry as well as physics during the 1940s. In 1940, Canadian-born American biochemist Martin Kamen discovered a radioactive form of carbon. Unlike normal carbon, whose nucleus contains 6 protons and 6 neutrons for a total of 12 nuclear particles, this radioactive carbon has 2 extra neutrons for a total of 14 particles. Therefore, it is called carbon-14. Kamen found that carbon-14 has a long half-life of 5,730 years. In other words, half the material will disintegrate in 5,730 years.

American scientist Willard Libby figured out a clever way to use carbon-14 to solve some baffling mysteries. Libby learned that the cosmic radiation that constantly showers the earth from outer space knocks protons and neutrons loose from atmospheric gases. Some of the free neutrons are then absorbed by nitrogen atoms. Nitrogen ordinarily has 7 protons and 7 neutrons for a total of 14 nuclear particles. When nitrogen absorbs an extra neutron, it becomes unstable. It kicks out a proton so that its atomic number returns to 14.

This reduces the nucleus to 6 protons and a total of 14 nuclear particles, which is the nuclear form of carbon-14. In other words, the nitrogen becomes carbon-14.

Working primarily alone on the project, Libby noted that plants convert carbon dioxide from the atmosphere into food and plant tissue during photosynthesis. He reasoned that some of this carbon must be in the form of radioactive carbon-14. Libby further found that carbon-14 breaks down in plants at the same rate at which it is absorbed.

When a plant dies, however, it no longer takes in carbon-14 through photosynthesis. Therefore, the amount of radioactive carbon in the plant will decline as the carbon disintegrates.

Like many scientists, Willard Libby spent most of World War II working on the Manhattan Project. It was then that he became intrigued with radioactivity.

Libby reasoned that, since the rate at which carbon-14 decays is known, a person could determine the age of a dead plant by measuring the amount of carbon-14 left in it. For example, since carbon-14 has a half-life of 5,730 years, if only half the original amount of carbon-14 is found in a plant, one can assume that 5,730 years have passed since the plant died. Even though only a tiny fraction of the carbon in a plant is carbon-14, the rate of decay can be measured with great precision by counting the particles that the radioactive carbon emits.

What is the use of measuring the age of dead plants? Dead plants have been used to make dwellings, paper on which to write, and fabric for clothing. If carbon-14 dating worked, it could determine how old these items were. That in turn would help archaeologists solve mysteries as to the age of various communities, villages, and tribes.

How Old Is This?

Libby put his method to the test by using it on a sample of an ancient Egyptian funeral boat whose age was known. Libby chopped up a sample and burned it to produce carbon gas. He funneled this into a Geiger counter that could measure the rate of radioactive decay. Libby's calculations came within 3 percent of the known age of the boat—3,750 years. The carbon-14 technique developed by Libby has since been perfected to provide even greater accuracy, up to 30,000 years.

Within a short time, carbon-14 dating became a standard tool of archaeologists in determining the age of artifacts they unearthed. Libby's pioneering efforts were eventually carried over into radioactive dating techniques that helped geologists determine the age of rocks and minerals. From this, scientists have been able to determine the age of fossils and various earth formations. Among their findings was the discovery that the earth is much older than originally supposed.

Libby proved that even great scientists can make great errors in judgment. During the 1950s, he dismissed fears that nuclear bomb testing was creating deadly poisons. According to Libby, "We really cannot say that testing is in any way likely to be dangerous. The test fallout [radioactive dust] is so small compared to the natural background."

Understanding Photosynthesis

Carbon-14 also played a role in an important discovery in biochemistry. American chemist Melvin Calvin used the material to solve a problem that had been baffling plant scientists for many years: how do plants manage to create plant tissue out of carbon dioxide, water, and sunlight?

Beginning in 1948, Calvin used carbon-14 to trace the path of carbon as it moved from an atmospheric gas into a plant's system. He fed radioactive carbon to a type of plant called algae. Calvin exposed some of the algae to light and kept some in the dark. Calvin then killed the plants and analyzed them, looking for chemical compounds within the plant that contained radioactive carbon. He then compared compounds formed in the photosynthesizing

Photosynthesis is a food-making process that occurs in green plants.

plants (the ones exposed to sunlight) with those found in plants that were kept in the dark. After several unsatisfactory attempts to explain the data, Calvin constructed his photosynthetic cycle. This explained in detail the chemical steps that occur in photosynthesis and the intermediate products that are formed in the complex process of converting carbon dioxide into glucose and oxygen.

HOW THE BODY USES IODINE AND CARBOHYDRATES

Chemists found other uses for mildly radioactive materials. In 1940, American scientist Herbert Evans used radioactive iodine as a "tracer." By measuring its radioactivity, Evans could trace the flow of iodine through the human body. In this way, he proved that iodine is needed for the thyroid gland to work properly.

Calvin's success in explaining photosynthesis was one of those unexplained flashes of brilliance that occur often in science. After accumulating a great deal of data, Calvin was stumped for an explanation of what he was seeing. While he was sitting at the wheel of his car, waiting for his wife to finish an errand, the answer suddenly jumped out at him. Calvin said, "I don't know what made me ready for it at that moment except that I didn't have anything else to do."

A further explanation of the chemical processes at work in biology occurred in the laboratories of German-born American biochemist Fritz Lipmann. In 1941, Lipmann explained how the human body gets energy from food. Lipmann found that as the molecules of carbohydrates are broken down, they combine with oxygen and phosphate to form phosphate bonds. These high-energy phosphate bonds are parceled out to the areas of the body where energy is consumed. Lipmann found that one phosphate bond in particular, adenosine triphosphate, is present and active in body chemistry at virtually every point at which energy is required.

HERBICIDES HELP THE AGRICULTURAL INDUSTRY

Chemistry came to the aid of farmers during the 1940s. During the 1930s, chemists had discovered poisonous chemicals that distinguished between the two major classes of plants. These chemicals prevented growth in broad-leafed plants but did not seriously disturb grasses. Fortunately for farmers, grain crops are all grasses, while many of the weeds that interfere with their growth are broad-leafed plants.

Armed with this knowledge, chemists in the 1940s produced commercial herbicides for use in agriculture. They developed the first effective herbicide, a compound by the chemical name of 2,4-dichlorophenoxyacetic acid, more commonly known as 2,4-D.

2,4-D was introduced widely during World War II. By the end of the war, chemical companies were producing nearly 1 million pounds (453,592 kilograms) of the substance per year. It proved so successful that by the end of the decade, farmers were using 14 million pounds (6,350,293 kilograms) per year.

PSYCHEDELIC STUFF

On a far different note, Swiss chemist Albert Hoffman made a bizarre and unexpected discovery while working with compounds from ergot, a highly toxic mold that grows on rye and wheat. During a 1943 experiment with a modified form of one of these compounds, Hoffman accidentally absorbed

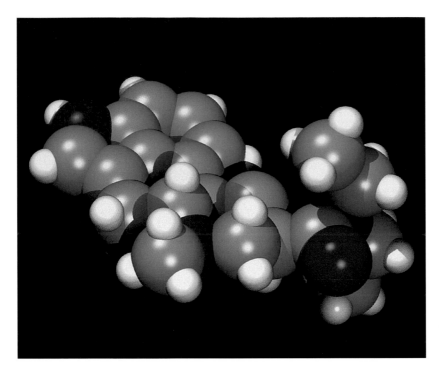

A computer-generated model of an LSD molecule

some. He suddenly began hallucinating. He began experiencing brilliant, swirling colors, powerful emotions, and bizarre images—almost like a dream or nightmare in vivid detail. Hoffman was the first person to "trip out" on lysergic acid diethylamide, more commonly known as LSD, a dangerous hallucinogenic drug.

3

BIOLOGY

George Beadle and Edward Tatum furthered the connection between biology and chemistry with their explorations into genetics, the science of how characteristics are passed on from one generation to another. Beadle and Tatum were interested in how the chromosomes, or the genes that made up the chromosomes, were able to cause certain characteristics to take shape in the new generation.

PASSING A TRAIT FROM ONE GENERATION TO THE NEXT

For their study, which they began in 1941, they chose to work with a red bread mold called *Neurospora crassa*. The mold was easy to grow and had the advantage of reproducing quickly so that they could study many generations in a short time. According to Beadle, "The best way to study the mystery of chromosomes was to find some mutation that affected the chemical behavior of the organism." With this in mind, the scientists tried to produce genetic mutations by bombarding the chromosomes with X rays.

Among the many mutations they produced were strains of mold whose individual cells were unable to form some of the organic compounds needed for growth. Beadle and Tatum found that they could provide the mold with similar compounds that would facilitate growth. They tried many different compounds to see which would promote growth and which would not. By analyzing differences and similarities in these compounds, they were able to discover which chemical reactions the mutated mold could no longer perform.

The scientists demonstrated that living things synthesize (make) the substances they require through long chains of chemical reactions that occur within the cells. They showed that the genes exert their influence over the new generation by regulating the individual steps in these chains of reactions. Beadle and Tatum concluded that each gene was responsible for the formation of a single enzyme.

THE IMPORTANCE OF DNA

The discovery that genes determine heredity by controlling cell chemistry helped found the new science of molecular biology. It opened the way for a new understanding of the chemistry of the body and shed light on the ways in which traits are passed on.

Oswald Avery, who began his career as a physician before going into biological research, pried open the mystery of heredity even further. He based his work on experiments performed by Frederick Griffith a number of years earlier. Griffith killed a strain of disease-causing bacteria and introduced it to a live, harmless strain of the same bacteria. Somehow the dead bacteria converted some of the harmless bacteria into disease-causing bacteria.

In 1932, Avery began studying what had taken place in Griffith's experiment. He knew that genetic material was located in thousands of genes that made up the chromosomes. He also knew that the chromosomes were made up of two kinds of giant molecules, protein and deoxyribonucleic acid (DNA). Most biologists believed that proteins were the key molecules that controlled genetic activity. After all, the enzymes that governed chemical activity in the body were proteins. No one knew what role DNA played, if any, in this activity. Some scientists believed it was an inert substance, sort of a filler.

Avery adapted much of Griffith's experiment in an

Oswald Avery worked to identify the specific carrier of inherited characteristics in all living things.

attempt to identify which molecule was responsible for passing on characteristics to the next generation. Working with pneumococci (bacteria that cause pneumonia), Avery isolated two strains. One was virulent (disease-causing) and the other nonvirulent. Avery found that the virulent strain had a smooth coat made from a complex carbohydrate molecule, and he labeled this the S strain. The other lacked this coat and had a rough surface; Avery named this the R strain. He observed that the R strain differed from the virulent S strain because it lacked the gene for creating the smooth coat.

Avery prepared extracts from the virulent strain and mixed them with the harmless R strain. Sure enough, one of these extracts converted the harmless R strain into virulent, smooth-coated pneumococci. Therefore, the extract that he used must have contained the gene for virulence. Avery then purified the extract and found that it was primarily composed not of protein but of DNA. He performed a great number of experiments over several years. By 1944, he was able to prove conclusively that the preparations most active in transmitting the S characteristic were the ones with the greatest concentration of DNA. Clearly, DNA was the specific carrier of hereditary characteristics in all living things.

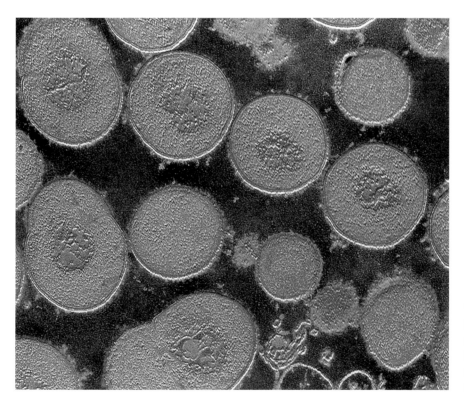

Oswald Avery's study of pneumonia-causing bacteria led to revolutionary advances in the study of genetics.

Avery was an extremely careful and conscientious scientist. He waited until two years after his discovery to publish his results while he meticulously checked to make sure all details of his experiments were accurate.

Avery's discovery revolutionized genetics. By pinpointing the unexpected source of genetic transmission, he provided scientists with the correct target at which to direct further studies. This led to the discovery of the chemical structure of DNA in the 1950s by James Watson and Francis Crick. Eventually, the information provided by Avery, Beadle, and Tatum led to the development of genetic engineering, which has almost endless potential for creating new and useful plants for food and other products, and possibly for reducing disease by isolating and altering genes responsible for defects and disease.

IMPROVING THE CHARACTERISTICS OF LIVESTOCK

While chemists came to the aid of crop-growing farmers in the 1940s with their pesticides, biologists introduced an important new technique to livestock farmers. In 1949, they discovered methods of freezing semen without damaging it. This made practical the technique of artificial insemination. Livestock producers have increasingly relied on this technique to improve efficiency in inseminating animals and to improve the quality of their livestock by obtaining semen from bulls with desirable characteristics.

4

COMMUNICATION AND
INFORMATION

While the creation of the atomic bomb dominated the scientific world of the 1940s, it had little direct effect on most people's lives. Nuclear power existed as a threat, a political reality, and a possible energy source. But to most people, it was and still is a far-off, mystical power that has not changed the conduct of their everyday affairs.

Science and technology of the 1940s brought far more dramatic changes to the average person in the areas of communication and information gathering. Few inventions of the twentieth century have altered a nation's lifestyle as thoroughly as the television, introduced to commercial markets in the 1940s.

TELEVISION COMES OF AGE

Most of the pioneering work with television had been done in the United States during the 1920s and 1930s. By 1940, engineers could transmit a recognizable, if grainy, image by camera to receivers many miles away. Enough bugs had been worked out of the system so that by 1941 the U.S. government approved the commercial sale of television sets.

However, only a few sets were sold before the United States became embroiled in World War II. A war crisis was no time to lavish money and effort on an entirely new industry devoted primarily to entertainment. Efforts to market television stopped while the fighting raged.

During the war, Vladimir Zworykin, the man primarily responsible for creating the television, kept working to improve television technology. Working for RCA, he succeeded in inventing a television camera one hundred times more sensitive than his previous efforts. By the end of the war, when American consumers were ready to take a closer look at this ingenious new device, Zworykin and RCA had a good product ready to show them, at a

Vladimir Zworykin's work on the discovery and development of television spanned several decades.

price that many Americans could afford. In the fall of 1946, they offered a black-and-white television set with a 10-inch (25-centimeter) picture screen.

Few new products have ever caught on so quickly. Americans bought 130,000 televisions in 1947. In the final year of the 1940s, more than 3.5 million sets were sold in the United States. Within a few more years, more than half the homes in the United States would have television, and the invention would find its way into homes in Europe as well. The television was well on its way to becoming one of the primary influences on modern culture, altering leisure time activities, political campaigns, sports, advertising, and even the way nations waged war.

Behind the scenes, new television technology was being devised even before the first sets were sold. In 1940, Hungarian-born American engineer/physicist Peter Goldmark found a way to transform the existing black-and-white images into color. Working for the Columbia Broadcasting System (CBS), Goldmark used a three-color rotating disk, which he successfully introduced in a 1940 broadcast. By the time commercial color television became available in the 1950s, however, Goldmark's system had been replaced by more effective color techniques.

Zworykin had a passion for scientific research. He envisioned his television as an educational and research tool, providing knowledge and images that would otherwise be unavailable to the world. He was disturbed by the entertainment industry's takeover of his invention for what he viewed as frivolous amusement. To the end of his life, he refused to watch commercial television shows.

More Music for Your Money

Goldmark had a longer-lasting influence in another corner of the entertainment industry—recording. During most of the 1940s, phonographs could only play records spinning at a high rate of speed: 78 revolutions per minute (78 rpm). Recording artists were generally able to get only one song on each side of a record. In 1948, Goldmark introduced the long-playing, or lp, phonograph system. By using narrower grooves on records and slowing the record speed to 33⅓ rpm, Goldmark increased the amount of what could be recorded by seven or eight times. This allowed consumers to listen to much longer musical pieces, such as symphonies, which was not possible with the old 78 rpm records.

Peter Goldmark (left) *at work developing a long-playing phonograph record*

I Want to See It—Now!

Another science-driven consumer product of the 1940s came about through the urgings of a three-year-old girl. In 1943, American inventor Edwin Land, founder of the Polaroid Corporation, took a vacation with his family in the Santa Fe, New Mexico, area. At one point during their sight-seeing, Land had his little daughter pose for a photograph. After Land snapped the picture, his daughter wanted to see the result—immediately! Land had to explain that developing a print was a long and complicated process and that she could not see the picture for several weeks.

Moved by his daughter's disappointment, Land wondered if there were some way to create a camera that could produce an instant print. At first, he only tinkered with some ideas in his spare time. But he became so intrigued with the challenge that by 1946 he was devoting most of his efforts to the project. So many obstacles stood in his way that Land had to come up with more than one hundred patented ideas before his camera became a reality.

In 1947, he unveiled his process to the world. Land used a double roll of film that contained the negative film and positive paper on which to make a print. Between these he placed sealed packets of chemicals. After the picture was taken, Land's camera released the chemicals and developed the print.

Even after Land explained his process, most photography experts thought it was an impractical gimmick. No company was interested in licensing his invention. Land had to go into the camera-manufacturing business himself and did very well selling his camera.

Edwin Land is shown here with an instant print—of himself!

AN INVENTOR AHEAD OF HIS TIME

Dennis Gabor, who also explored the world of photographic images, did not design any consumer product. In fact, he was so far ahead of his time that no practical use could be made of his invention for more than fifteen years after he conceived it. But it was during the 1940s that Gabor developed the idea of holography, perhaps the most important development in optical sciences in the twentieth century.

Gabor was yet another Eastern European scientist who found his way to

Gabor's moment of inspiration was remarkably similar to Melvin Calvin's. The basic idea of holography struck him while he was sitting on a bench, waiting for his turn on a tennis court.

the United States during political turmoil. During the years immediately following World War II, he was involved in research with the recently invented electron microscope. This machine could magnify tiny images far better than ordinary light microscopes. Gabor's task was to solve some minor problems in creating a clear picture with the electron microscope.

During his experiments, Gabor observed that ordinary photography consisted of having a beam of light reflect off an object onto photographic film. This recorded a flat, two-dimensional image of the object. Gabor wondered what would happen if the beam of light were split in two and both halves of the beam aimed at an object. Both halves would be reflected back to the film. When the film was developed, a light passed through it would cause it to produce a three-dimensional image. Because this process would capture all three dimensions instead of only two, Gabor called the process holography, which means "whole writing."

Gabor worked out his entire theory in 1947. But in order to be effective, the beam that was split had to be "coherent" light. Unlike ordinary light from a light-bulb, which includes many different wavelengths of light, coherent light consists of only one wavelength of light. At that time, there was no way to produce a coherent light beam strong enough to make the process practical. That had to wait for the invention of the laser in the late 1950s and 1960s.

Dennis Gabor was awarded the Nobel Prize in physics in 1971 for a process he had worked out theoretically decades earlier.

The first hologram was created in 1965. Holography has since become more widely used, not only as a novelty item and in three-dimensional films, but also in industry to test products for defects and deformities. For example, holography checks the strength of the bonds between layers of rubber tires.

THE COMING OF THE COMPUTER

Another scientific development of the 1940s that would radically alter the modern world several decades in the future was the computer. Oddly, World War II had the effect of both squelching and promoting computer development. In 1942, Americans John Atanasoff and Clifford Berry built their ABC computing machine, which was a forerunner of modern computers. They had not actually gotten their device fully operational, however, before they were called to work on other wartime projects. Before they could get back to their computer work, others had passed them by.

Among those who advanced the technology of computers was a British group headed by mathematician Alan Turing. Using vacuum tubes as the basic operating parts of the machine, they created the Colossus, which was designed specifically to crack Nazi Germany's horrendously complex Enigma code. The Colossus succeeded. Confident that their code could never be broken, the Germans were free in their use of Enigma. They did not worry about their transmissions being intercepted, since they thought no one else could understand them. The fact that Great Britain and its allies could read top secret German communications and could therefore prepare for much of what the Germans planned to do was a key factor in the outcome of the war.

Another computer pioneer was Howard Aiken, who had proposed his Automatic Sequence Controlled Calculator back in 1937. Working at Harvard University on a joint effort with the International Business Machines (IBM) company, Aiken produced the Mark I. More than 750,000 parts and 530 miles (853 kilometers) of wire went into making the Mark I. In January 1943, the machine passed its initial test by correctly solving a problem given to it. The Mark I, which was programmed with punched paper tape, was the first computer that effectively performed its job for a long period of time. The machine, which was capable of multiplying two eleven-digit numbers in approximately three seconds, functioned for nearly fifteen years.

According to computer lore, the Mark I contributed the term *debugging* to popular scientific vocabulary. Once when the computer stopped functioning for a time, Aiken came in to see what the problem was. Technicians told him that the malfunction was caused by a moth that had flown into the computer and that the Mark I would be up and running once they had debugged it.

Aiken originally envisioned the Mark I as a one-of-a-kind machine to solve complicated problems that would normally take a person weeks or even months to perform. But the Mark I was barely into production when a growing demand for computers sparked competitors that passed it up. During World War II, the United States' Ballistic Research Laboratory in Aberdeen, Maryland, was responsible for producing mathematical tables to tell gunners what angle of trajectory to use for firing their weapons at certain distances. With all the new artillery being designed for the war, the lab was falling far behind in updating these tables.

To their rescue came John Mauchly and John Eckart Jr. with the ENIAC, the first all-electric, all-purpose stored program computer. Unfortunately, the machine was not completed until after the war ended. But it performed many useful functions for the government during its nine-year life.

Technicians working on the enormous ENIAC computer

The main problem with computers at this point was their monstrous size. The ENIAC, for example, weighed 30 tons (27 metric tons) and consumed 1,500 square feet (135 square meters) of floor space, as much as exists in the average house. The computer was also an energy hog. So much electricity was required to run the ENIAC's thousands of vacuum tubes that the lights in a nearby town dimmed every time the machine was turned on.

Computers of the 1940s also had problems with reliability, mainly because vacuum tubes frequently wore out and had to be replaced. The computers also gave off a great deal of heat.

The bottom line was that even the best computers were barely worth the expense and effort of building and running them. Computers seemed destined to be exotic machines, useful only to a few well-financed, specialized operators.

SEMICONDUCTORS AND TRANSISTORS

However, the 1940s also brought about an invention that would one day make computers practical enough to operate in the home. Typical of the 1940s, the invention had a war connection. While doing research for materials to use in the creation of radar for the war, British and American scientists studied the characteristics of materials such as germanium and silicon (the primary component of ordinary sand). These materials were known as semiconductors. Semiconductors are solid substances that neither conduct electricity nor stop its flow—they do some of both. At the end of the war, the Bell Research Laboratories took on a multimillion-dollar study of semiconductors.

The Bell project was basically a fishing expedition for new materials that could be used to improve their electrical products. The company had no product in mind when it started the research. In an example of the high esteem that industry held for science because of its recent accomplishments, the company was willing to make a huge investment on the *hope* that exploration of a new field of study might turn up something useful.

William Shockley, who headed the project for Bell, found semiconductors intriguing because there was no logical explanation for why a material could both conduct and insulate. The mystery became even more baffling when his research team found that an electrical field did not have the predicted effect on the material's conductivity.

The Bell team found that a semiconductor's efficiency in conducting varied with many factors, including the amount of impurities in the material. Eventually, they figured out that these impurities freed a certain number of electrons to move about and conduct electricity. The researchers saw that if they could find a way to control this movement of electrons, they would have a useful product for the electronics industry.

In a series of experiments performed late in 1947, Shockley and colleagues John Bardeen and Walter Brattain created a device that could adjust impurities in semiconductors to create the desired flow of electrons. They attached three metal contacts to different areas of a specially prepared germanium chip. The electrical current flowing between two of the contacts could be controlled by the voltage applied to the third. The Bell team called this device a transistor, which is short for "transfer of resistance."

Transistors proved to be important because they could perform the same function as vacuum tubes, without the disadvantages. Unlike the glass vacuum tubes, transistors did not break easily or wear out. They took up only a fraction of the space and used a fraction of the power of vacuum tubes. Since transistors could be made out of silicon, one of the more common elements in the world, they could be made cheaply.

Because of their ability to amplify electrical signals, transistors were quickly adapted for use in small, lightweight, portable radios and in hearing aids. Transistors eventually made possible a whole world of miniaturization that turned bulky, unwieldy contraptions into streamlined, practical products.

One of the main benefactors of this miniaturization has been the computer. Because the thousands of glass vacuum tubes could be replaced by tiny silicon transistors, computers eventually shrank from the size of a gymnasium to something that could fit on a desk.

As computers became practical, they began to revolutionize the way modern society processes information. Word processing functions of computers have replaced the typewriter in modern offices. The mathematical cal-

The Bell Company eagerly announced its breakthrough during a press conference on June 30, 1948. But almost no one in the media understood the importance of the discovery and it received scant attention.

John Bardeen (left), *William Shockley* (center), *and Walter Brattain* (right) *were winners of the Nobel Prize in physics in 1956 for the invention of the transistor.*

culations performed by computers have made possible everything from moon exploration to massive government programs such as Medicare and Social Security. The boom in computer technology that occurred during the 1940s has accelerated to the point where astounding computer innovations become obsolete almost as soon as they hit the market.

A SCIENCE FICTION STAR IS BORN

In 1945, the seeds of another scientific breakthrough in communication were sown, not in a laboratory but in a magazine office. While serving in Great Britain's Royal Air Force during the war, Arthur C. Clarke had been assigned to work in a radar unit. His fascination with this new technology sparked a creative interest in imagining what other marvelous machines might be on the horizon. Clarke became a science fiction writer. (He is best known for writing *2001: A Space Odyssey*, which was published in 1968.)

In 1945, Clarke wrote a magazine article in which he proposed the idea of a satellite that could reflect signals sent from one continent to receivers across the ocean. Twenty years later, fact caught up with fiction as the first communications satellites were launched into space. They have become the primary means of rapid communication between continents.

5
TRANSPORTATION

During the 1930s, Auguste Piccard's work carried him in the opposite direction of his dreams. The Swiss professor of mechanical engineering spent most of the decade launching balloons that carried him and his colleagues higher above ground than any person had ever traveled before.

UNDER THE SEA

But Piccard's heart was not in the sky but rather in the ocean. Ever since he had been a young boy, his dream had been to "plunge into the sea deeper than any man before." Following a 1937 flight, Piccard abandoned his balloon efforts and focused on building a vessel that could take him to the uncharted depths.

The war interrupted his plans and it was not until the late 1940s that Piccard made real progress. Prior to that time, others had descended into the ocean in diving bells lowered by cable from a ship. Piccard wanted something that could move around deep beneath the surface. Submarines did not suit his purpose because they could not withstand the crushing pressures of deep water.

Piccard built a diving ship along the same lines as his famous balloons. The upper portion was a cigar-shaped float filled with gasoline (which is lighter than water) to give the ship buoyancy. The bottom part was a sturdy metal sphere, much like the stationary bathyspheres already in use. Small electronic propellers provided the power to move under the surface of the water. Piccard called his invention a bathyscaphe, which means "ship of the deep."

The bathyscaphe was filled with heavy iron pellets. The ship could descend by replacing some of the gasoline in the float with heavier seawater. It could return to the surface by discarding the heavy iron pellets.

Piccard built his first bathyscaphe in 1948. Initial tests did not go well. He reached a depth of 4,500 feet (1,372 meters), far short of his goal. But after many years of adjustments, the same ship descended to a world record of 10,168 feet (3,099 meters) in 1953. Seven years later, it journeyed to the bottom of the deepest part of the ocean—the Marianas Trench, which lies 35,800 feet (10,912 meters), or nearly 7 miles (11 kilometers) below the surface.

THE AMAZING JACQUES COUSTEAU

One of Piccard's assistants in his diving efforts was a small, wiry French naval officer named Jacques Cousteau. Cousteau had been an amateur ocean diver prior to World War II. At that time, divers required a heavy suit and a lifeline that pumped air to them. This greatly restricted the mobility of the diver, who had to stay within the limits of the lifeline and take care that it did not become entangled.

When the Germans occupied France during the war, Cousteau joined the French underground resistance to continue the fight against Germany. While with the resistance, he developed the Aqua-Lung, a device that replaced a diver's clumsy lifeline. Cousteau simply supplied the diver with a lightweight tank containing compressed air. This freed the diver to explore tight places such as caves and coral reefs and to wander far from a base ship without fear of cutting the lifeline. Cousteau's innovation was useful in sabotaging enemy ships. After the war, it made exploration far more practical for undersea buffs. It led to greater exploration and understanding of the vast undersea world.

Jacques Cousteau has made the study of the sea and its creatures his life's work.

Cousteau's invention became known as scuba. *Scuba* is an acronym for <u>s</u>elf-<u>c</u>ontained <u>u</u>nder-water <u>b</u>reathing <u>a</u>pparatus.

INTO THE AIR

The quest for high-speed travel proceeded on two fronts in the 1940s: rockets and jet airplanes. Jet propulsion was already a reality at the beginning of the decade, its progress accelerated by war needs. In late summer of 1939, German test pilots completed brief flights in experimental aircraft models. Germany began a full-scale effort to produce jet fighter planes in late 1941.

Great Britain fell two years behind Germany in jet airplane development. Successful trials with the Gloster-Whittle turbojet engine were not conducted until 1941. But British engineers made up for lost time. By the summer of 1944, Gloster Meteor jets roared into the sky, about the same time that German Me 262 jets appeared. Both planes could fly faster than any propeller-driven plane, attaining speeds of more than 500 miles (805 kilometers) per hour. Germany put even more effort into production, manufacturing more than one thousand Me 262s. But the war in Europe was already winding down by the time these aircraft were ready, and they had little effect on the war's outcome.

Even while German jet planes moved into production, a report prepared for the United States government dismissed the notion of jet air flight as impractical.

ROCKET SCIENCE

At the same time that they were designing jet aircraft, the Germans also made huge strides in rocket science. They had this field virtually to themselves, thanks to American neglect of inventor Robert Goddard. Goddard, a professor at Clark University in Massachusetts, had pioneered rocket research back in the 1920s. His accomplishments were largely ignored and even scorned. That neglect continued when Goddard offered to help his country develop a rocket as a weapon during World War II. Thanks but no thanks, he was told.

The Germans, however, were paying attention. When Adolf Hitler approved government-sponsored rocket research in 1936, much of that effort proceeded along the lines Goddard had established. Wernher von Braun, son of a German baron, directed the project. Germany invested a huge amount of time, effort, and money in rocket science. By the end of the war, the staff at the German experimental rocket station at Peenemünde on the Baltic Sea had grown to more than 20,000.

At first, the Germans tried to adapt von Braun's rocket engines to use as superpowered aircraft. In 1939, they launched an experimental rocket-powered plane on a fifty-second flight. That led to the development of the Me 163 rocket-fighter. However, so many German pilots died or were seriously injured flying the explosive, temperamental aircraft that Germany switched its emphasis to rocket-powered missiles instead.

Wernher von Braun made major contributions to Germany's rocket program. He came to the United States following World War II and was part of many of the successful space programs at the National Aeronautics and Space Administration (NASA) until his retirement in 1972.

By 1942, they had built the world's first true missile, a self-propelled shell carrying its own fuel supply and explosives. Called the V-1, this missile could fly at 466 miles (750 kilometers) per hour, about as fast as a fighter plane.

Militarily, the V-1 was a dud. Although Germany fired thousands of these at London, few ever reached their target. British radar could locate the missiles in flight and fast British fighter planes could intercept and destroy them with ease. During one missile attack, the British intercepted 97 of 101 V-1 missiles launched.

Two years later, Germany developed a truly terrifying missile—the V-2. This projectile stood 40 feet (12 meters) high and weighed more than 28,000 pounds (12,700 kilograms). Great Britain had no chance to defend itself as these giant missiles came screaming across the English Channel at more than 3,500 miles (5,635 kilometers) per hour. Of the 4,300 V-2s launched, 1,230 hit London, causing more than 2,500 deaths.

As with the jet engine, however, Germany's rockets came too late to be a major factor in the war. With its defeat, Germany forfeited its wide lead in rocket technology to the victors. The United States recruited von Braun to assume control of its rocket program, designed for peaceful as well as military purposes. In 1946, the United States launched a rocket carrying a spectroscope. The rocket soared 50 miles (80 kilometers) into the air, at which

A V-2 rocket lying on a freight car. U.S. Army troops captured a V-2 production plant in 1945, putting a stop to the plant's production of nearly 900 V-2 rockets per month.

point the spectroscope took photographs of the sun, free of lower atmospheric interference. Three years later, American scientists at White Sands, New Mexico, put a small rocket on top of a captured V-2 rocket. After the large rocket burned out, the smaller rocket ignited. It kept going until it reached a distance of 240 miles (386 kilometers) above the earth. This concept of a multistage rocket eventually carried astronauts to the moon and sent rockets traveling millions of miles into the solar system.

But while rocket technology helped scientists conquer new worlds, it also increased world tensions. The United States and Soviet Union soon placed nuclear warheads on rockets that could be launched at their targets from hundreds, even thousands, of miles away.

CAN THIS BARRIER BE BROKEN?

As jet and rocket engines boosted aircraft speed during World War II, pilots discovered a frightening phenomenon known as the sound barrier. At lower speeds, air molecules easily pass over the wings and nose of a plane, allowing it to pass smoothly. But these air particles cannot move faster than the speed of sound (around 700 miles, or 1,127 kilometers, per hour, depending on the altitude and temperature). When the plane approaches this speed, the air cannot get out of the way fast enough. It piles up in front of the plane. This causes severe vibrations and stress.

Pilots had many colorful descriptions of what this did to an airplane. One fast-flying pilot said he "started sliding through the air as if on ice." Another likened his experience to "flying straw in a hurricane." Even the best aircraft engineers in the early 1940s were not confident it was possible to design an airplane that could handle this stress and break the sound barrier.

The danger and uncertainty of the sound barrier did not stop pilots and engineers from trying to break it. German pilot Rudolf Opitz, flying an Me 163B Komet, reached a top speed just over 700 miles (1,127 kilometers) per hour in 1944. The turbulence at that speed threw his plane out of control. As it plunged toward the Baltic Sea, the thicker atmosphere at low altitude slowed the plane enough for him to regain control just as it was about to hit the water. In late 1946, British pilot Geoffrey DeHavilland Jr.'s DH 108 Swallow was ripped to pieces by turbulence after reaching speeds in excess of 600 miles (965 kilometers) per hour.

*Chuck Yeager,
the man who broke
the sound barrier
in 1947*

Embarrassed by its tardy start in jet and rocket research, the United States made a determined effort to break the sound barrier. Engineers designed a bullet-shaped plane with razor-thin wings to accomplish the task. This aircraft, called the X-1, was powered by a rocket engine fueled by an explosive mixture of liquid oxygen and alcohol.

During 1947, the X-1 inched closer to the sound barrier. The pilot chosen to guide the aircraft through the barrier was Chuck Yeager, an air force pilot from West Virginia. As Yeager tested the X-1 at higher and higher speeds, however, he began to experience heavy buffeting and lack of control. Yeager and his superiors began to believe that the sound barrier was too powerful to surmount.

But Yeager's friend, a brilliant engineer named Jack Ridley, scoffed at fears of the sound barrier. "The only barrier is bad aerodynamics and bad planning," said Ridley. Ridley studied the problem and made some minor adjustments that helped stabilize the X-1.

On October 14, 1947, a B-29 bomber carried the X-1 to 20,000 feet (6,096 meters) over a remote area of California. Yeager climbed into the cockpit of the X-1. The B-29 dropped the smaller plane into the sky. "My heart was in my mouth and my stomach right behind it," said Yeager.

Yeager needed an incredible streak of luck to earn fame as the pilot who broke the sound barrier. Chalmers "Slick" Goodlin was slated to fly the X-1 past the sound barrier. But as the trials progressed, Goodlin held out for more money. The air force promptly dumped him and brought in Yeager. Then, during a test run, Yeager broke the rules by trying some hotdog stunt flying with the X-1. He had to apologize hard and fast to keep angry officials from booting him off the job. Finally, he broke some ribs falling off a horse just before the record-breaking flight. Had his superiors known of his injuries, they would not have allowed him to fly, but Yeager never let on.

Yeager fired the rockets and the X-1 shot up into the sky. As he approached the speed of sound, he found the usual unnerving barrier waiting for him. Shock waves began to shake and batter the aircraft. But as the X-1 continued to accelerate, the buffeting eased. The world's first sonic boom echoed over the California desert. Yeager had broken the sound barrier.

Because of concerns about keeping military technology a secret, the air force suppressed news of the supersonic flight for many months. Although rumors of the flight spread across the country, the air force waited until June of 1948 to confirm the information.

Yeager shrugged off his contribution to the historic event. "It was just a matter of flying the airplane," he said. Although that is a modest exaggeration, the shattering of the sound barrier was primarily a triumph of science and engineering.

6

SPACE AND THE UPPER ATMOSPHERE

In the 1920s, Edwin Hubble had confirmed earlier conjecture that the entire universe was expanding. Astronomers were faced with the problem of explaining why this was so. The most likely explanation was that the universe had long ago been compressed into a small space and then had undergone a gigantic explosion. Perhaps this explosion had created the universe.

PONDERING THE EARLY MOMENTS OF THE UNIVERSE

In the 1940s, Russian-born American George Gamow was puzzling over this problem. Gamow was yet another link between the fantasy world of science fiction and the reality of science. His father was a professor of literature, and George wrote and illustrated popular books on science.

Gamow was looking for some explanation of how the heavier elements in the universe were formed. There did not seem to be any evidence to indicate that such elements were continually being formed. So Gamow wondered whether these elements were created in the early moments of the universe, when the universe was extremely dense and hot.

Using his calculations as their basis, Gamow and his colleagues Ralph Alpher and Robert Herman proposed that the universe began at a single, almost infinitely small point, a billion times smaller than the area of a single proton. This incredibly hot, dense matter exploded. As it expanded, neutrons immediately started to expand and decay into protons and electrons. These formed in various combinations that made up the heavier elements.

Gamow and his colleagues calculated that, because of the extreme heat required for this process, most of these elements were formed in the first minutes after the birth of the universe, before the rapid expansion and cooling of the universe made this impossible. The universe had been expanding

George Gamow, one of the principal advocates of the big bang theory

and cooling for so long that now the average temperature of the universe was just a few degrees above absolute zero.

Gamow calculated that this so-called big bang birth of the universe should have produced a surge of energy. If this had happened, then there should still be some background microwave radiation produced by this ancient surge coming equally from all parts of the sky.

Gamow had no way of measuring whether or not such a thing as cosmic radiation existed, and so could not test his claim. But in 1964, two radio

Gamow had a sense of humor that got him into trouble when his paper on the origin of the elements was published. Noting that his name and Ralph Alpher's were similar to the first and third letters of the Greek alphabet (alpha and gamma), Gamow signed on astronomer Hans Bethe as a contributor to his paper against Bethe's wishes, beta being the second letter of the Greek alphabet. This made the authors of the paper Alpher, Bethe, and Gamow, and it became known as the ABC paper. Many scientists thought inclusion of Bethe just to make a pun was unprofessional.

astronomers began using a powerful new antenna that picked up stray noise. The astronomers were puzzled by this at first, but eventually they concluded that it was the cosmic radiation predicted by Gamow. This discovery provided strong evidence of Gamow's claim that the universe was born at a specific time in a superhot, big bang explosion.

SURPRISES IN THE UPPER ATMOSPHERE

While Gamow and radio astronomers were dealing with the unfathomable reaches beyond the earth, others discovered a surprising phenomenon in a more accessible area of the sky. Some scientists had suspected as early as the 1920s that strong winds unlike anything found at ground level might exist in the upper atmosphere. World War II pilots, cruising at higher altitudes than anyone had flown at before, found out the hard way that they were right.

In November of 1944, the United States launched Operation San Antonio, a strategy of bombing Japanese war industries in Tokyo from high altitude. American B-29 bombers were assigned to drop their loads from about 30,000 feet (9,144 meters). While relatively safe from enemy fire at such an altitude, the pilots found themselves battling a fierce gale. According to a military report, the "tremendous winds encountered at bombing altitude over Japan offered a novel and disconcerting problem." The bombers could not fly safely into the teeth of the 200-mile- (322-kilometer-) per hour winds flowing from west to east. Nor could they place their bombs accurately while being whisked along by such a fierce tailwind. The American military had no choice but to switch to lower-level bombing tactics.

The American pilots had run into one of several bands of high wind in the upper atmosphere, hundreds of miles wide and several miles deep. These winds were capable of velocities in excess of 300 miles (482 kilometers) per hour. By 1945, meteorologists recognized that these winds, which they called jet streams, were a permanent feature of the atmosphere and had a profound effect on the weather and climate of the earth.

One wave of one hundred B-29s sent out in November of 1944 failed miserably in their attempt to carry out Operation San Antonio. Due to high winds, the bombers managed to damage only 1 percent of the target buildings.

Knowledge of the existence of jet streams radically changed the science of meteorology. Thanks to the work of Swedish-born American meteorologist Carl-Gustaf Rossby, scientists learned what causes these jet streams, how they move, and how they affect conditions down on the ground. The result was a consistent, marked improvement in the accuracy of weather forecasting. Improved forecasting reliability has not only proved useful in planning events but has saved lives.

7
HEALTH AND MEDICINE

Prior to the 1940s, almost all increases in life expectancy had come from a greater awareness of public health measures. As governments took steps to ensure clean water and safe food and to route sewage away from contact with people, and as people learned of the connection between germs and illness, public health improved.

The 1940s marked a shift toward dependence on science and technology to fight disease and alleviate other health problems. Scientific research produced a vaccine against yellow fever, which saved the lives of thousands of soldiers sent overseas during World War II. Large-scale production of DDT during the 1940s probably saved millions of lives. The chemical prevented epidemics of malaria and typhus by killing the mosquitoes and body lice that carried these diseases.

But the decade's most remarkable lifesaving accomplishment was the development of antibiotics—drugs that could kill disease-causing bacteria without harming the patient.

ADVANCING THE STUDY OF ANTIBIOTICS

As early as the late nineteenth century, microbiologists had found that certain bacteria were capable of destroying other bacteria. They had seen a number of cases in which one bacteria colony overwhelmed and wiped out another bacteria colony. The question was: how were the bacteria doing it? Were they producing some kind of toxin that was harmful only to certain types of bacteria? If so, perhaps some of these toxins would kill disease-carrying bacteria while causing no harm to the human body.

Since then, scientists had been unsuccessful in their search for a useful selective toxin, with a couple of exceptions. In 1907, German Paul Ehrlich had found a chemical dye that killed the protozoans that caused sleeping sickness and later found a compound that destroyed bacteria that caused syphilis. In 1932, another German, Gerhard Domagk, discovered the first sulfa drug. These chemicals did not actually kill bacteria; they deprived them of nutrients. This often weakened the bacteria so that the body's immune system could fight them more effectively.

But as the 1940s dawned, sulfa drugs were proving to be inadequate. They were ineffective against many types of infections, especially severe infections. Medical researchers began to doubt that it was worthwhile continuing the frustrating search for inexpensive, safe drugs that could stop dangerous infections cold.

A Discovery in Dirt

In 1939, however, French-born American microbiologist René Dubos found that *Bacillus brevis*, a bacterium that lived in the soil, produced a mild toxin that worked against other bacteria. Dubos was able to isolate and purify this toxin, called tyrothricin. This substance could kill some forms of bacteria without causing serious harm to other creatures.

Tyrothricin was not the miracle antibiotic medical researchers had been hoping for. It was only mildly effective against harmful bacteria yet was not safe enough to be taken internally. But its discovery encouraged researchers. Here was proof that there really were antibacterial agents in nature that attacked only certain bacteria.

Dubos's discovery rekindled efforts to find new, more effective antibiotics. The threat of world war at the end of the 1930s, which had the potential of causing thousands of gaping wounds vulnerable to fatal infection, made this research even more urgent.

The Possibilities of Penicillin

Among those who joined the search was Australian-born British pathologist Howard Florey at Oxford University in England. Working with Ernst Chain, another refugee scientist from Germany, Florey decided to conduct tests on a long list of antibacterial substances produced by bacteria and mold. It so happened that one of the first three candidates he chose for his screening in 1939 was penicillin, a substance produced by the mold *Penicillium notatum.*

This mold's antibiotic powers had been accidentally discovered by Alexander Fleming of Great Britain back in 1928. After seeing how well it killed bacteria, Fleming had thought it might be useful as a local antiseptic to prevent open wounds from becoming infected. But he never thought seriously about the possibility of using it as a medicine. He had never even tried to give the mold to mice. Furthermore, he was never able to purify the penicillin. Eventually, he quit working with the material, and no one paid much attention to penicillin until Florey and Chain came across a report of Fleming's experiment during their search for antibiotic candidates.

Although Alexander Fleming discovered penicillin in 1928, commercial production of this antibiotic did not occur until World War II.

Florey and Chain decided to begin their survey with penicillin. Unlike Fleming, Chain had the biochemical training to purify the substance without loss of effectiveness. When the researchers administered the pure drug to eight mice infected with streptococcus bacteria in May of 1940, they found they had hit the jackpot. Penicillin was so incredibly potent in fighting disease that it continued to kill bacteria even when diluted to one part in two

Fleming owed his success to a poorly run experiment in which he allowed a bacteria culture to become contaminated with, as it turned out, penicillium. According to Ernst Chain, Fleming's lack of attention to detail was typical. "No one who knew Fleming would call him a tidy bacteriologist," Chain remarked.

million! Florey and Chain saw no further need to continue their search. Instead, they focused all their efforts on studying this material.

In 1941, the researchers began testing penicillin in humans. They found it effective in killing bacteria without harming patients. Penicillin's first human test case was a London police officer seriously ill from an infection of a cut he sustained while shaving. The drug produced a startling improvement, but not enough of it was available to finish the job. The officer died.

The problem was that patients had to take a continuous supply of penicillin over several days in order to achieve success. Scientists had difficulty producing the relatively large amounts required. Florey was able to obtain 1,000 units of penicillin per liter of fluid produced by the mold. This was about one-hundredth the daily dosage needed for humans. Florey would have to process about 2,000 liters (528 gallons) of the cultured fluid in order to treat one human case.

Florey and Chain tried to scale up production but were hampered by lack of facilities. At one point, they were using enamel bedpans as containers for growing mold. There were many obstacles that stood in the way of producing large amounts of penicillin. As one expert remarked, "The yields are low, isolation is tough, extraction is murder, and purification invites disaster."

Locked in a struggle for survival with Nazi Germany, Great Britain did not have the resources to spare on gearing up industrial-scale production of penicillin. Florey traveled to the United States, where researchers were safe from fighting and had greater resources to work with. He and others persuaded American researchers to take up the cause of penicillin production.

Because of the medical importance of penicillin, United States pharmaceutical companies joined together to find ways to increase production. The cooperative effort produced astounding results. American companies produced 400 million units of penicillin in the first five months of 1943. By the

The first American patient to use penicillin was Mrs. Ogden Miller, a thirty-three-year-old woman dying of severe strep infection. The drug gave her a complete and speedy recovery. When word of this miracle medication spread, people with critically ill relatives became desperate to get some of the limited supplies.

end of the year, they had increased production by more than fifty times. When the Allies launched their invasion of Normandy in June of 1944, they had all the penicillin they needed to treat disease and serious infections of battle injuries among soldiers. By the following summer, American companies were churning out 650 billion units of penicillin per month.

Few single achievements in science have had such a dramatic impact on human life as the discovery and development of penicillin. From 1945 to 1955, the number of deaths from influenza and pneumonia in the United States fell by 47 percent.

DIGGING TO DISCOVER STREPTOMYCIN

René Dubos's discovery of bacteria-fighting tyrothricin in soil microorganisms and the rediscovery of penicillin spurred renewed interest in antibiotics. Russian-born American microbiologist Selman Waksman had been Dubos's teacher, and his student's discovery motivated him to get in on the action.

Working at Rutgers University in New Jersey, Waksman undertook an effort similar to what Florey had proposed: a systematic testing of soil organisms for antibiotic compounds. With few funds to support his work, Waksman had to use simple screening techniques. But in 1940, he found an antibacterial compound in the soil fungus *Streptomyces griseus*. This substance, which he called streptomycin, destroyed some harmful bacteria that penicillin could not. In 1946, researchers at the Mayo Clinic in Minnesota showed it to be effective in combating tuberculosis. Streptomycin, however, was much more toxic than penicillin and had to be used carefully.

It was Waksman who first used the term *antibiotic* to describe substances that attacked bacteria without harming the host. Waksman was enchanted with the teeming microscopic activity of the soil. "Young man, there is romance even in a manure pile," he told one of his students. Waksman liked to quote a phrase from the Bible, "out of the earth shall come thy salvation," to illustrate his firm belief that the study of soil microorganisms was crucial to life. He was genuinely humbled by the realization that his discovery saved many lives.

More Antibiotics

Yet another type of antibiotic came about through the research of Benjamin Dugger of the University of Wisconsin. In 1944, Dugger, an expert on plant diseases, discovered Aureomycin. This was the first of a class of drugs known as tetracycline, which often work more effectively and with fewer side effects than other antibiotics.

Taken together, the antibiotics developed in the 1940s have had a profound impact on world health. Many illnesses and infections that formerly caused death could now be cured completely in a matter of days. Deaths from bacterial infection, which as recently as the early nineteenth century was the leading cause of death among humans, have since become rare in industrial societies.

Scientists were able to make great strides in the bacterial wars because they could easily grow and study these microorganisms. They did not have the same luxury with another source of disease—viruses. Viruses would only grow on living cells. This made laboratory work with them expensive and difficult. During the 1930s, scientists made a breakthrough in virus research when they discovered how to grow viruses in chicken eggs or embryo cells. This eventually led to a vaccine against yellow fever that saved countless soldiers' lives during World War II.

Viruses and Vaccines

But scientists continued to have trouble keeping bacteria from contaminating these virus cultures. The development in the 1940s of antibiotics such as penicillin that would kill bacteria and not harm viruses solved that problem.

A team of American researchers led by John Enders set about perfecting new methods of growing viruses with the aid of penicillin to keep bacteria in

Enders's career showed the effect a single influential teacher can have on a person's life. Enders had no particular interest in science as a young man. After a failed attempt to go into business, he enrolled at Harvard University with plans to become an English teacher. But he was so inspired by a microbiology teacher named Hans Zinsser that he switched to microbiology.

68

check. They concentrated their work on mumps and measles viruses. Progress was slow and painstaking but eventually they succeeded in growing the mumps virus on mashed chicken embryos.

At the conclusion of their experiments, they had some leftover scraps of chicken embryo. Instead of discarding this material, they tried to find a way to make use of it. They decided to see if they could grow poliovirus on the tissue.

Polio was one of the most pressing concerns of virologists (scientists who study viruses) in the 1940s. The disease was crippling thousands of children and young adults every year. One had to look no further than U.S. President Franklin Roosevelt, who could not walk unassisted, for evidence of the damage polio could do.

Researchers had tried to come up with a vaccine for polio in the 1930s. The problem with the poliovirus, however, was that virologists were able to grow it only in nerve tissue. Viruses grown on nerve tissue were difficult to tame. Indeed, the viral vaccine created in the 1930s proved about as dangerous as the disease.

In 1948, Enders surprised virologists by growing the poliovirus not in nerve tissue but in muscle and skin tissue from embryos. His team also discovered an easy way to detect the growth of viruses, which were too small to be seen even with an ordinary microscope. They used a dye to detect the presence of an acid produced by healthy tissue. If the level of acid declined or was absent, the virus was thriving.

These advances opened the way for the possibility of developing a safe polio vaccine, which Jonas Salk eventually accom-

After contracting polio in 1921, Franklin Delano Roosevelt could no longer walk unaided. He rarely permitted photographs that showed his leg braces or that showed him walking with crutches.

plished in 1954. The vaccine almost immediately erased the threat of polio. At its peak in 1955, more than 58,000 new cases of polio appeared in the United States. Within a few years of the development of the polio vaccine, the disease was well on its way to complete elimination.

TOLERATING A TRANSPLANT

Several breakthroughs of the 1940s opened the door for a new medical technique—transplanting healthy tissue and organs into a human body to replace those that were unable to function. Prior to this time, attempts to make transplants failed because the human body's immune system is programmed to attack foreign proteins, such as the transplanted material.

Australian Frank Burnet wondered why the body's immune system did not attack its own proteins. How did it learn to identify foreign protein from "self" protein? Burnet noted that some immune reactions can be developed or stimulated. That indicated that these immune reactions were not inborn and unchangeable. Burnet proposed that embryos do not have all these immune reactions. At that early stage, the body learns to recognize, or develops a tolerance for, the substances that are present so that it will not mistake them for harmful foreign invaders at a later date. Burnet's ideas proved to be correct.

George Snell added to this knowledge of the mechanisms of tolerance and rejection by showing that tolerance and acceptance of foreign proteins were governed by genetics. Working with laboratory mice, he located the sites of specific genes that were concerned with acceptance and rejection.

Understanding the mechanisms of

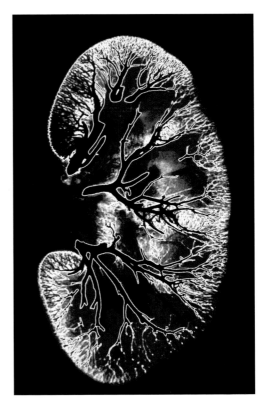

The kidneys are essential organs that filter waste out of the bloodstream. The development of the first artificial kidney in 1943 was a revolutionary development in medicine.

rejection and tolerance made it possible for researchers to find ways of creating conditions in which the body would accept transplanted material. Medical researchers made this knowledge practical by devising artificial organs. In 1943, Dutch-born American physician Willem Kolff designed the first artificial kidney.

UNDERSTANDING THE RH FACTOR

Karl Landsteiner worked out a solution for a specific kind of rejection. In 1940, he and physician Alexander Wiener injected red blood cells from a monkey into a rabbit. They were surprised to discover that the same antibodies in the rabbit that attacked these monkey cells also attacked some human cells. The researchers concluded that rhesus monkeys and humans have similar protein in their red blood cells.

The scientists called this protein Rh factor (named after rhesus, the type of monkey used in the experiment). Knowledge of this blood marker has saved the lives of countless children. A fetus whose father is Rh-positive (has this protein) and whose mother is Rh-negative (does not have it) can cause the mother to produce antibodies against the Rh protein. That means that in future pregnancies, the mother's antibodies may attack the fetal cells, resulting in anemia, jaundice, brain damage, and sometimes death. Because they understand the effect and the reactions of the Rh factor, doctors can now prevent these problems before they occur.

The discovery of the Rh factor, a protein in red blood cells, led to a dramatic decline in the number of infant deaths due to Rh disease.

NEW HOPE FOR THE MENTALLY ILL

The 1940s brought the first effective medical treatment for mental illness. Until that time, no one knew how to treat the wild mood swings of manic-depressive people or the bizarre behavior of schizophrenics. French neurosurgeon Henri Laborit made the initial breakthrough when he used an antihistamine called promethazine to calm patients prior to using anesthetics. When this proved mildly promising, he experimented with an even stronger drug, chlorpromazine.

Upon Laborit's recommendation, psychologists Jean Delay and Pierre Deniker used chlorpromazine to treat patients in the highly excitable stage of manic-depression. The quieting effect was remarkable. Within a decade, mental health professionals in Europe and the United States routinely used chlorpromazine to treat both manic-depressive and schizophrenic patients.

Meanwhile, John Cade, a young psychologist working at a small hospital in Australia, began injecting lithium salt into guinea pigs. His experiments showed that lithium could be used to effectively treat mania.

Cade believed that manic-depression was caused by the patient's inability to metabolize uric acid and that lithium could correct this deficiency. He was wrong about the link between uric acid processing and manic-depression. Nevertheless, for reasons that remain unclear to this day, lithium has been an effective treatment.

Since Cade worked in a remote Australian town and published his findings in an obscure Australian medical journal, word of his success with lithium treatment spread slowly. But eventually, the use of chlorpromazine and lithium triggered a major shift in the way society dealt with mental illness. Prior to the 1940s, authorities simply warehoused hundreds of thousands of mentally ill patients who were considered too dangerous to be allowed to roam free. Thanks to the new drugs, the numbers of psychiatric patients in state mental hospitals declined 75 percent in the 1950s, and even further in the 1960s.

While chlorpromazine calmed patients, its success overstimulated a few imaginations. Some professionals expressed the belief in scientific publications that chlorpromazine could end or at least greatly curtail juvenile delinquency.

A New Kind of Birth Control

Finally, Russell Marker, a chemistry professor at Pennsylvania State College, unwittingly started a cultural revolution with his research on progesterone. This sex hormone used to treat menstrual disorders was extremely expensive.

Marker found that he could produce progesterone from a chemical compound known as diosgenin. This seemed of little practical importance because diosgenin was also rare and expensive. But then Marker discovered that wild yams in the tropics of Mexico were loaded with diosgenin. Working without outside financial support, he rented a laboratory in Mexico City and collected 10 tons (9 metric tons) of yams.

After easily extracting diosgenin worth $2,270 per ounce ($80 per gram), he persuaded a small Mexican company to go into large-scale production. Before long, this company put so much diosgenin on the market that the price dropped to less than $57 per ounce ($2 per gram). This made research on progesterone practical.

Researchers in the 1940s found that the hormone inhibited ovulation and therefore could be used to prevent unwanted pregnancies. Progesterone, however, had to be injected every day to be effective, which made it an impractical birth control solution. That quickly changed later in the decade when scientists discovered chemical forms of the drug that remained stable in the stomach and could be taken internally. By the 1960s, these oral contraceptives were refined enough to put on the market. The effects of this new, easy method of birth control were enormous and widespread. It helped bring about changing attitudes toward women's rights, brought about increasing debate among religious groups, and provided a tool for combating what many scientists believed was the foremost long-range problem of humanity—overpopulation.

Further Reading

Aaseng, Nathan. *Twentieth Century Inventors*. New York: Facts on File, 1991.

Asimov, Isaac, *How Did We Find Out About Computers?* New York: Walker and Co., 1984.

Balcziak, B. *Television*. Vero Beach, Florida: Rourke, 1989.

Black, Wallace B., and Jean F. Blashfield. *Hiroshima and the Atomic Bomb*. New York: Macmillan, 1993.

Burge, Michael C. *Vaccines: Preventing Disease*. San Diego: Lucent Books, 1992.

Calabro, Marian. *Zap! A Brief History of Television*. New York: Macmillan, 1992.

Cousteau Society Staff. *An Adventure in the Amazon*. New York: Simon and Schuster, 1992.

Driemen, J. E. *Robert Oppenheimer: Atomic Dawn*. New York: Macmillan, 1988.

Facklam, Howard, and Margery Facklam. *Viruses*. New York: Twenty-First Century Books, 1994.

Farris, John. *Hiroshima*. San Diego: Lucent Books, 1990.

Graham, Ian. *Lasers and Holograms*. New York: Franklin Watts, 1991.

Hoff, Mary, and Mary M. Rodgers. *Our Endangered Planet: Population Growth*. Minneapolis: Lerner, 1991.

Jervis, Alastair. *Camera Technology*. New York: Franklin Watts, 1991.

Kaye, Judith. *The Life of Alexander Fleming*. New York: Twenty-First Century Books, 1993.

Lampton, Christopher. *Rocketry: From Goddard to Space Travel*. New York: Franklin Watts, 1988.

Larsen, Rebecca. *Oppenheimer and the Atomic Bomb*. New York: Franklin Watts, 1988.

Liptak, Karen. *Dating Dinosaurs and Other Old Things*. Brookfield, Conn.: Millbrook Press, 1989.

McGowen, Tom. *Radioactivity: From the Curies to the Atomic Age*. New York: Franklin Watts, 1988.

McPartland, Scott. *Edwin Land*. Vero Beach, Fla.: Rourke, 1993.

Milne, Lorus J., and Margery Milne. *Understanding Radioactivity*. New York: Macmillan, 1989.

Newton, David E. *Population: Too Many People?* Hillside, N.J.: Enslow, 1992.

O'Neal, Michael. *President Truman and the Atomic Bomb: Opposing Viewpoints*. San Diego: Greenhaven, 1990.

Reef, Catherine. *Jacques Cousteau: Champion of the Sea*. New York: Twenty-First Century Books, 1992.

Sherrow, Victoria. *Hiroshima*. New York: Macmillan, 1994.

Steffens, Bradley. *Phonograph: Sound on Disk*. San Diego: Lucent Books, 1992.

Streissguth, Tom. *Rocket Man: The Story of Robert Goddard*. Minneapolis: Carolrhoda, 1995.

Tames, Richard. *Alexander Fleming*. New York, Franklin Watts, 1990.

Wilcox, Frank H. *DNA: The Thread of Life*. Minneapolis: Lerner, 1988.

Index

References to illustrations are listed in *italic, boldface* type.

Abelson, Philip, 20, 21
Aiken, Howard, 46–47
airplanes, 9, 10, 12, 53, 55, 56–58
Allies, 9, 24, 46, 67
Alpher, Ralph, 59
antibiotics, 12, 63–70
arms race, 27–28
atoms, 10, 12, 15
    combining, 26–27
    splitting, 15, 16, 18–20, 26
Avery, Oswald, 38, *38*, 39–40

bacteria, 38, 39, *39*, 64. *See also* antibiotics.
Bardeen, John, 49, *50*
bathyscaphe, 51–52
Beadle, George, 37, 40
big bang theory, 59–61
biology, 37–40
bombs, atomic, 10, 11, 17, *24*, 41
    construction of, 23–24
    moral issues involving, 25–26, 27
    nuclear, 17, 33
    producing, 20, 21, 22
    use of, 24–26

bombs, hydrogen (thermonuclear), 26–28, *28*, 29
Brattain, Walter, 49, *50*
Burnet, Frank, 70

Cade, John, 72
Calvin, Melvin, 33–34
cameras, 41, 43–44
carbon–14 (radioactive), 31–32, 33
Chadwick, James, 15
Chain, Ernst, 64–66
chain reactions, nuclear, 16, 17–19, 20, 22, 23, 26
Clarke, Arthur C., 50
Compton, Arthur, 20, 24
computers, 9, 12, 46–48, 49–50
Cousteau, Jacques, 52, *52*, 53
Crick, Francis, 40
critical mass, 19, 23

decay, radioactive, 32, 33
diffusion, 20–21, 22
DNA (deoxyribonucleic acid), 38–40
drugs
    antihistamines, 72
    lithium, 72
    oral contraceptives, 73
    penicillin, 64–67

streptomycin, 67
sulfa, 64
tetracycline, 68
Dubos, René, 64, 67
Dugger, Benjamin, 68

Eckart, John Jr., 47
Einstein, Albert, 17
electricity, 10, 13, 49
electrons, 49, 59
elements, 15, 16, 23
    discovery of, 21, 22
    origin of, 59–60
Enders, John, 68–69
energy
    atomic, 12, 16, 26
    nuclear, 15, 41
engines, 53, 55, 56, 57
ENIAC, 47, *47*, 48
Enola Gay, 24–25, *25*
Evans, Herbert, 34

Fermi, Enrico, 15–18, *18*, 19–20, 21, 24,
    27
fission, nuclear, 16, 17–18, 19, 26, 27
Fleming, Alexander, 65, *65*
Florey, Howard, 64–66, 67
fusion, nuclear, 26–27

Gabor, Dennis, 44–45, *45*, 46
Gamow, George, 59–60, *60*, 61
Geiger counter, 19, *22*, 33
genetics, 12, 37–40, 70
germanium, 48, 49
Goddard, Robert, 53, 54
Goldmark, Peter, 42, 43, *43*

Hahn, Otto, 15–16

half–life, 31, 32
heredity, 37–40
Herman, Robert, 59
Hiroshima, Japan, 25, 26
Hoffman, Albert, 35–36
holography, 44–46

jet streams, 61–62
Joliot–Curie, Frédéric and Irène, 15, 16,
    16, 17

Kamen, Martin, 31
kidneys, *70*, 71
Kolff, Willem, 71

Laborit, Henry, 72
Land, Edwin, 43–44, *44*
Landsteiner, Karl, 71
Lawrence, Ernest, 15, 21, 24
Leopold, Aldo, 13
Libby, Willard, 31–32, *32*, 33
LSD (lysergic acid diethylamide), 36,
    36

Manhattan Project, 11, 12, 18–24
Marker, Russell, 73
Mauchly, John, 47
McMillan, Edwin, 21
Meitner, Lise, 16
mental illness, treatment for, 71–73
microorganisms, 64, 67, 68
military, 17, 24, 27, 61
missiles, 9, 54–55
molecules, 38–39, 56

Nagasaki, Japan, 25, *26*
neutrons, 20, 59
    bombardment with, 16, 21, 23

and critical mass, 18, 19
and radioactive elements, 31
as subatomic particles, 15

Oak Ridge National Laboratory, 20, *21*
Oppenheimer, J. Robert, 17, 23, 24, 25, 27, 28
organ transplants, 70–71
outer space, 26, 31, 50, 59–62

particles
   nuclear, 31, 32
   of matter, 10, 59
   subatomic, 15
penicillin, 64–67, 68
phonograph system, long–playing (lp), 12, 43
photography, 43–46
photosynthesis, 31, 33–34
physics, 10, 15–29, 31
Piccard, Auguste, 51
plants, 12, 31, 33–34, *34*, 35, 40, 68
plutonium, 22, 23–25, 26
pneumococci, 39, *39*
polio, 69–70
power, nuclear, 10, 13, 15, 17, 23, 41

radar, 9, 10, 17, 48, 50
radiation, 21, 31, 60–61
radioactivity, 15, 19, 31, 34
red blood cells, 71, *71*
Rh factor, 71
Ridley, Jack, 57
rockets, 53–55, *55*, 56, 57, 58
Roosevelt, Franklin, 69, *69*
Rossby, Carl–Gustaf, 62

Salk, Jonas, 69–70

scuba, 52–53
Seaborg, Glenn, 22, *22*, 23
semiconductors, 12, 48–49
Shockley, William, 48–49, *50*
Snell, George, 70
sound barrier, 56–58
"suicide squad", 19, *19*
Szilard, Leo, 17

Tatum, Edward, 37, 40
technology, 9, 13, 41, 46, 63
television, 12, 41–42
Teller, Edward, *27*, 28–29
Tibbets, Paul, *25*
transistors, 12, 49
Truman, Harry, 25, 26, 28
tryothricin, 64, 67

universe, formation of, 59–61
uranium, 15–16, 18–19, 20–21, 22–23
Urey, Harold, 20

vaccines, 63, 68–70
Velcro, 11, *11*
viruses, 68–70
von Braun, Wernher, 54, *54*, 55

Waksman, Selman, 67
Watson, James, 40
Weil, George, 19,*19*
Wiener, Alexander, 71
World War II, 9–13, 35, 46, 47, 52, 61, 63, 68. *See also* Allies; bombs, atomic; rockets.

Yeager, Chuck, 57, *57*, 58

Zworykin, Vladimir, 41–42, *42*

About the Author

Nathan Aaseng attended Luther College in Iowa and earned a B.A. degree with majors in both English and biology. He was particularly interested in the communication of scientific information to general audiences. After working for four years as a research microbiologist, he turned to writing full time.

Mr. Aaseng has written more than 100 books, primarily nonfiction for younger readers. He currently lives in Eau Claire, Wisconsin, with his wife and four children.